S0-BXW-828

Yo, Alejandro

The Story of a Young Latino Boy
Struggling Through Life

Alejandro Gac Artigas

Ediciones Nuevo Espacio
Second Edition, March, 2001

Yo, Alejandro

Cover: Melina Gac-Artigas
Ediciones Nuevo Espacio
New Jersey, 07704 USA
http://www.editorial-ene.com
ednuevoespacio@aol.com
First Edition, November, 2000
Second Edition, March, 2001
ISBN: 1-930879-21-0

For all those who have once sat on the
benches of life.

Para todos los niños que alguna vez
se han quedado sentados
en el banco de la vida.

Acknowledgements

I would like to express my gratitude towards the two people who honored me by first reading my manuscript: a literature teacher, Mr. Stephen Michaud, and my Language Arts teacher in eighth grade, Miss. Vanessa Kabash.

Thanks for your kind words and encouragement.

MY FIRST BREATHS

Though I do not remember, I was told by my sister that my birth was accompanied by great gusts of wind, uncommon in The Netherlands. So great and ferocious were these winds, that as my father and sister left the hospital in which I was born, our van, a heavy yet translucent blue shade, had evanesced into the horizon.

On October the 22nd of the year 1988, I received both my first breath of air, and my first admonition of the capricious and arduous life I was to lead.

THE CAMPUS DAYCARE

Not long after my life commenced I was enrolled in what was called The Campus Daycare. This particular daycare sat deep in the heart of The West Georgia College, which was in fact quite convenient for at the moment my mother gave lectures merely 50 yards yonder. Those were times in which you accomplished something that was seen as difficult for your age and, most importantly, you were applauded with the equivalent fervor and adulation as received by other children.

As I first entered The Campus Daycare, having recently arrived from Puerto Rico, I knew but a word of English and had but one thought in mind: success, my mouth accustomed to *hola's*, and *si's*, and *la raza*.

My learning of English happened without me even acknowledging I was unearthing a completely different language; all I knew was that if I wanted to be understood I needed to use the same words they spoke. Perhaps other children felt the same way about my Spanish, who knows? At first our communication was brief, much as an infant with a desire yet without the ability to express it by voice. Little by little I realized the English translation for *zanahoria* was carrot and not *zanorate;* with *chaquet* (derived from *chaqueta*), my English version of jacket, I was much closer; and as my first year in The United States concluded, I spoke English as well as anyone else in the class.

THE DAY I MET THE GORILLAS

I remember the day our teachers had decided to escort us to the zoo, giving a long tour of sights and lectures. At the zoo we viewed animals whom our teachers had previously stated were walking freely in a completely natural and open habitat. As it was eight years in the past, and I was only 3 ½, I among others believed it.

The first thing I saw as I entered the zoo were bars. Beyond the supposedly pleased animals I beheld a child who posed to be a great discrepancy. This particular boy was united with his mother not by affection nor trust, yet by an exceedingly short leash, of a partially crimson and golden shade, as if a slave, or docile pet.

I am still bewildered, presently, at the fact that such a small instrument can dismantle such an eminent privilege: freedom. At the moment I saw that boy I developed a concrete yet indescribable sense of protection for my given privileges. Simply put, I did not desire to find myself in the situation or in a similar situation as to what I had recently witnessed.

Meanwhile, being absorbed by the leashed boy, the tour proceeded without me, having not noticed my absence. So as to once again be alongside my classmates, and to exercise my freedom, I now decided to traverse the cage in which were gorillas, and to perhaps say hello.

Beside me there was a massive wall, a barrier to prevent any child from attempting what I was preparing to perform. (Now that I recall the actual size of the wall, it was, in reality, quite small, yet seemed large to my eyes, for, as I told you, at the time I was 3 ½ and the wall reached well over my waist.) Upon seeing the wall I realized that we, my classmates and I, had as little freedom as the animals, for this great wall was our own "bars." My small fingers, barely able to grasp anything larger than a brick, reached over the wall and pulled. And so my first and second attempts failed. I glanced at the leashed boy and at my class, and with renewed strength ascended the wall.

The second obstacle of my venture proved quite easy. As a result of my size, I was able to fit in between the bars. Though I did not process the fact in my mind, there was no longer a barrier in between the gorillas and I. At approximately the same moment as when I entered the cage, the teacher who was allegedly watching over me acknowledged I was missing, and later froze, her face an expressionless pale mask, for she had spotted me among the gorillas.

The little boy on the leash tugged avidly, attempting to follow behind me. I now felt like a mixture of Tarzan and Pied Piper. Almost instantly the entire zoo had quieted and stared, mouths wide open, at my place in the cage, as if playing roles in a silent film. I almost was led to believe I had seen Charlie Chaplin standing to the right of my teacher.

I found it quite amusing to see how calm the gorillas seemed in comparison to the surrounding public. The gorillas approached me. I approached the gorillas. At about the center of the cage we converged, our two worlds had met. The largest and closest ape, whom I supposed was the leader, placed his nose in the thick air and sniffed me, as if to say hello. I returned the greeting in the same manner. No words were spoken.

Succeeding my brief moments among the gorillas, I left the cage with perhaps the greatest memory of my life, and still yet, in the present, nothing has relegated the experience, and still yet the ape has my utmost respect. Some call my encounter a miracle. I call it a conversation in silence.

As I took my first step once again upon the beaten dusty path there was a great exhale, as if by the entire world. I was no longer Tarzan nor Pied Piper, I was just

Alejandro although in my soul I will always be the two characters that existed in the cage that day. Miss Jill, my teacher, dropped on her knees and embraced me, a tear falling down her pale cheek. She would later tell me not to speak of this to my parents, frightened of what their reaction might be.

It was not until I wrote this book that they learned of the astonishing experience. The telling of the story to my parents made me fall in laughter, for their face was the same face Miss Jill had while I was in the cage, they wore the same pale mask, their mouths wide open.

THE TOWER
OF THE CAMPUS DAYCARE

The Campus Daycare stood to be one story tall, being simply an extremely large room sitting by a playground and toy shed. Built within seven square feet, on the right corner stood the Tower of The Campus Daycare. This particular tower was nothing but an elevated porch in appearance, yet in its history and in its arms it held the memories of many other children similar to us who have cherished this tower as much as we did.

To rest upon that tower a child must have been of age four, and be in their last year at the daycare before graduation towards kindergarten, or must have accomplished a deed that none other had done. Of course these were only the solemn rules and regulations of the children, and in not long, because of the adults' disapproval, the bottom half of the tower, our tower, was open to all those who attended the daycare. This half contained a quite large, wooden trunk, looking as if it had been recently pulled out from the ocean after years of being lost at sea. Within the trunk lay an array of clothing and costumes that had come to accumulate a great deal of dust. Laying alongside the chest was a mirror, also bathed in dust and cobwebs. Neither the teachers nor the children bothered to clean it, for we were fond of it as it was.

Also on the bottom half of the tower were intriguing novels, composed mainly of large pictures and small words, and though no one could read them they made us feel quite adult-like indeed. When the teachers found time, in between cleaning stains from the now leathery worn carpet or returning toys to their proper places, they read the books aloud.

Our class enjoyed parables, myths, and adventures, such as Tom Sawyer. I, being one of the most eager children in the class to be an intelligent adult, longed to be given the privilege to ascend the moaning ladder leading to the top balcony, the most elevated spot in the entire Campus Daycare, the most prominent sanctuary of our minuscule worlds . . . and to accomplish this I must perform a deed so uniquely spontaneous that I would be found on a third level if there were one.

BICYCLES

As my second year at the Campus Daycare concluded, one of the most difficult tasks of a lifetime was bestowed upon me: attempting to ride a bicycle. It was in this year that my father had bought two second-hand bikes, a worn, utterly pink one for my sister, without the presence of training wheels, and a slightly more lustrous red bicycle for me.

I was very pleased with myself for my bike was identical to my sister's, with the exception of color and size. This sense of being an adult soon evanesced as I saw my father installing training wheels. As a 3½ year old there was nothing I wanted more than being an adult, which was about seven at the time, and so, training wheels did not seem as sophisticated as I would have liked.

In fact, the previous day at the daycare one of my classmates, Lucas, had ridden his bicycle with training wheels and was worshiped by the Daycare, for he had been the first to put the tricycle in the past and purchased a bicycle. It was this that inspired me to be upon but two wheels, half the number of the wheels Lucas had ridden on and twice the difficulty.

The Campus Daycare had supplied us students with small tractors powered by pedals and tricycles and balls that bounced and pogo-balls and all sorts of toys, yet none as difficult as the bicycle. In other words we were given four wheelers, and three wheelers, and no wheelers, yet none as difficult as the two wheeler, none as difficult as the bike.

At the time, there was no greater accomplishment nor greater challenge than having the ability to ride a bicycle, and I desired that feeling of joy and pride it gives. I now had a bike yet lacked the ability to ride it, so I asked my father to teach me. With not much time on his hands he first was doubtful he could, yet after seeing my gleaming, desperate eyes he agreed. My father, mother, sister, and I left the apartment we rented and walked to a nearby parking lot in which I first felt like a truly accomplished adult.

At first my father held on to the back of my bicycle seat and was forced, by me, to promise not to let go. I was petrified, almost unable to pedal, clutching the handlebars as if for my life. (I would later partially regret this, for afterwards my small hands ached for a week, yet my pride extinguished pain.) In not long papi, as we called my father with a deep Spanish accent, saw my legs in motion and released his grip on the seat of the bicycle at the point were I began. I had not noticed and continued to pedal. As I neared the point were papi let go I didn't know whether to be frightened or whether to laugh, or whether to continue or whether to stop, yet that all did not matter . . . I was riding a bicycle.

The following day at the Campus Daycare I told my classmates of my achievement, and of course no one believed it. Being that most of the children had not yet even learned to ride a bicycle with training wheels, I later recognized they had reason to not believe, yet they would no longer have reason to doubt my accomplishment if they themselves had seen it with both their inquisitive eyes.

As I returned from the daycare, a bit disappointed, I asked my father to bring my bike to the campus of the college so I would have evidence proving I had not lied, and I was able to move astride a two wheeler. His reply was yes, and so brought my bicycle to the school as the day concluded. Papi had offered to once again hold on to the seat of the bike, yet I rebuffed his remark, simply saying, "I'd like you to, but my pride won't allow it." He understood and stepped back as a spectator.

The moment I removed the small red

bicycle from the back seat of our worn yet venerable Ford some children laughed at the second-hand bike, which I cherished as a treasure, and they viewed as a rusted ball of metal. Now they no longer laugh, for that day I had ridden my bicycle with but two wheels and though they may have had bikes of more color or luster, and for that matter price, my ability had now made my bicycle priceless, far more than all the money and riches they had.

At approximately the same hour the next day, I lay both asleep and content on the top balcony of the Campus Daycare.

MY FATHER, PAPI

Papi has been a tall heavily built man since I can remember. A beard penetrates the skin on his chin, which is now increasingly grayish and stiff. I always seemed to find comfort putting my head against his, so I felt his breath, and burying my cheek deep into his beard.

The moment I fell into his arms my problems were obscured into oblivion. The few moments upon his lap seemed enough to renew my strength and to prepare me for the troubles of life, for though at the time were rare, existed.

MY MOTHER, MAMI

My mother was of greater patience than my father. She was more lenient and understanding, and though perhaps obstinate and a bit opinionated, always in my benefit. Throughout the past years she has been supportive and for the most part correct. It was she who partially influenced the making of this book, for without her I may have corrupted into the wrath I was confronted with.

MY FIRST PIANO

I had always desired to play the piano, since the moment I first heard Alicia de la Rocha play. On a particularly warm day in August, in fact, sufficiently sultry to actually fry an egg upon the red asphalt of the track, where going outside was a burden and risk, I sat on our old flower-patterned couch, waving my fingers in mid-air, as if playing the piano. I was unaware that in but brief moments I would feel keys beneath my fingers.

My parents had bought a fairly thin, only approximately a foot in depth, brown piano for merely one hundred five dollars. It was worn smooth by much use, for just as the bicycle, this was second-hand also. Carved upon the wooden frame and body were pillars covered by vines and cherubs whose detail had faded.

The piano was anomalously tall, and the keys sounded a bit stifled and out of tune. It appeared as if it should be sitting in a corner near the stage of an old bar, having a beer mug on its top, with a middle-aged man, wearing a striped blouse with a black band about the upper arm, a cigar hanging from his mouth, and a twisted visor upon his head, playing rag and singing to accompany a performance.

I was forced to place a telephone book on the bench to play the keys, yet could no longer reach the pedals. Melina, my sister, reached the pedals with only the tips of her toes, for she was much older, seven at the time.

A previous owner of the piano had written the letter of the note which each key sung. Being that we had no knowledge nor experience of playing the piano, we simply played the keys that seemed correct, closed our eyes, and attempted to hear the music we desired. We would at times cross our hands, spin around, and lift our toes but centimeters away from the keys to appear as if we had utmost talent.

In not long, my parents could no longer bear to hear our dissonance and lack of noticeable talent, and so the search for a piano teacher began.

MRS. CULPEPPER

In Carrollton most piano instructors did not accept children under the age of eight, which posed to be a great problem, for both my sister and I were under the set age. Melina had turned seven, and I was nearing the age of four. As we came upon our seventh request for a piano teacher, a woman who taught at the College, told us that she also believed we were too young to be taught the piano.

My parents were a bit sad for a short while, yet not discouraged; they are not the kind of parents who give up easily, much less when it deals with our education. The instructor whom we last asked did in fact tell them about a well-educated young teacher, a dear friend and colleague of hers, and so she became our last opportunity before returning to pelting aimlessly the keys on the piano. Her name was Mrs. Culpepper.

My parents called Mrs. Culpepper upon notice, fearing to be told the same answer spoken by each piano instructor we knew of, yet she did not, stating in her cordial, affable voice that she believed age was not at all what mattered, that capability and, most importantly, eagerness to learn and practice were the two necessary factors to create a well-playing piano student. She wanted to perform an assessment to make the final decision as to whether we were prepared to play the piano.

Unlike most of the other instructors we had met, Mrs. Culpepper was young and had fine features. She had red hair, which hung a trifle above her shoulders, and was noticeably more amiable than the great majority of adults. As we neared her house to attend our assessment I heard music unlike anything I had ever heard in real life and upon the curtains saw the shadow of Mrs. Culpepper's fingers moving rapidly up and down along the keys of the piano. At that moment I thought with great determination that I must enter her class, for it was like her that I wished to play.

Mrs. Culpepper opened the door, and greeted us kind-heartedly. She asked us which one of us was to be first to take the exam. In a small, childish voice I rapidly and instinctively said, "Melina." Before Melina was able to speak, Mrs. Culpepper had already led her to the bench of her piano and begun to speak while correctly positioning Melina's hands on the keys. Meanwhile, I was hiding behind the bushes in front of her house, in a game I would perform throughout the three years in which I was her student.

When Melina had successfully passed the assessment, my parents began to ponder whether she would also be willing to teach me, while Mrs. Culpepper sought my position and finally took me inside. She sat at the bench close to me and made me repeat the notes she played on the piano. After what I remember as ten or fifteen minutes she conferred with my parents in a far-off isolated corner where eavesdropping was not possible, and told me to join my sister outside.

In my heart I was fearing that she would deny my request, yet became quite confident when I saw the faces of my parents but minutes later. At that moment I realized that I was in fact grateful and not resentful of my age, for I now was going to be taught by the teacher I knew was the best.

It was not as simple as I thought it was going to be, as what I had imagined; in order to learn to play I had to learn to recognize which letters and numerals corresponded to each note, and, as primary as it may seem, to remember which was the right hand and which was the left, for each hand would play differing notes. Mrs. Culpepper created flashcards which I thoroughly and avidly studied each night with my mother, mami.

I began to progress in both my ability and love of the piano. Mrs. Culpepper had taught me to play the piano perhaps better than any other instructor could, and I cherished her company. I began studying the piano in August of 1992, two months before my fourth birthday. In January of the same year my sister was to play a piece selected by Mrs. Culpepper, one she would play for the recital in June.

I was quite disappointed and indignant when she did not give me an additional piece to play and practice in preparation for the recital, but I didn't dare to ask why I was not to play. Was she angry at me? Was she dissatisfied with my work, or perhaps it should not be referred to as work, after all it had not provided me with the honor of playing in the recital? Was I not practicing enough? Was I not sufficiently talented for performing at the recital? Did people not want to hear my music?

All these questions turned around and around inside my head, but I didn't ask; I simply continued practicing and practicing and I promised to myself, that I would play at the recital to show Mrs. Culpepper I could.

What I did not know was that Mrs. Culpepper never thought I was not capable of performing or was not pleased with my form of playing. The only reason she had not assigned me a piece to play in the recital was that she believed I was going to be intimidated by the audience and did not want me to be exposed to the situation.

After seeing my partially discouraged and yet partially determined face as I played, my parents told Mrs. Culpepper that I had been practicing for hours and was convinced that my name was going to be upon the pages of the recital's brochure. They felt that not placing me in the recital may create a sense of dejection which could therefore banish both my desire and will to play the piano. She explained to my parents her fear, but they, having known me longer, reassured her that I was not easily intimidated and so she gregariously agreed to include my performance in the recital.

I will never forget the day of the recital nor the extolling words of praise and pride for my accomplishments and work with which Mrs. Culpepper introduced me. She sat by my side on the bench of the piano, to make it seem as if any other lesson, and I played the song which I had practiced for months. It was not a classical piece, as I had imagined when she first mentioned the recital, yet it little mattered, for I was there, at the recital playing my first piece in public, making my first appearance as a piano student, a renowned song entitled "Old

MacDonald" which received the admiration and applause of all the younger brothers and sisters of the children that were performing that day.

When I finished, I bowed, as Mrs. Culpepper had taught me, and as a four year old I ran to my parents' arms. I remember my parents' eyes full of tears of joy and Mrs. Culpepper's illuminated face.

Mrs. Culpepper now has a cancerous tumor. I sincerely wish she lives to see this message: I will never forget you, for even if I may not see you, you will always be with me in my heart. Thank you for wonderful memories.

"I'M SORRY, BUT IT IS THE LAW"

By teaching me the numbers and the letters of notes Mrs. Culpepper was not only preparing me to play the piano, but for the education of the world I neared: elementary school. After a second year in the Campus Daycare the students were promoted to kindergarten, so the last semester was pure anxiety for both parents and children, for we were about to take a large step in our lives as students: progressing to kindergarten and attending the "big school".

I was as eager as the other students, perhaps more, to go to "the real school." The school in which you must study more than play; the school in which you were required to learn a great deal more than we ever had. And so that night I slept with the books with which I had started to learn to read, in which I had drawn my first *palotes*, long straight lines, some embellished with round bellies, their purpose to help in the learning of cursive.

The next day I learned the Campus Daycare had received the list of students accepted to enter kindergarten . . . my name was not there. At first I simply believed it was an error, and asked Miss. Jill, and then Miss. Kim, yet they both said they did not have the authority nor knowledge to answer, and so I went directly to Mrs. Amanda, the director of the Campus Daycare.

Mrs. Amanda told me not to worry, that my parents would explain to me later. From that moment on, the other children at the daycare looked at me as "inferior" for being the only one not going to the "big school" which implied that I had to stay one more year with the "babies". I was no longer "one of them". Soon, I no longer rested upon the second level of the tower. I had lost all I had strived for in my time in America, and broke down to tears.

When my parents came to pick me up from the daycare I read in their faces, and they read in mine, that something was terribly wrong. I immediately asked them if I was to go to the "big school" next year. They hugged me very tightly and said, "Yes, Alejandro, you will go to the big school, we promise, you will go to the big school next year." The confidence they attempted to display with their gestures reassured me, yet in their eyes I saw the reality. My parents themselves were not assured that the promise was rightful, the only thing they were certain of was that if it must be, there was going to be a great battle.

Carrollton Elementary or Mrs. Neal's school, as we used to call it, for Mrs. Neal was the principal's name, was a newly created, quite large school. It was a "pilot school," a school experimenting new curricula and activities, part of the project "schools 2000" in which the state of Georgia built to prepare students for the year 2000.

The building was composed of six wings of classrooms connected at the center with what were the administration offices. It was a massive school with an immense, tremendous cafeteria, a computer room, a music room with a piano, keyboards, and other instruments, and an art room. Many new programs were added to the curriculum: Spanish, Art, and enrichment classes.

It was the school of one's dreams, and so when I went with my parents to register they gave me extensive exams to see how well prepared I was for attending kindergarten, and to see if I was able to attend the school.

I answered each question given to me correctly, with the exception of the final question: The woman giving the oral exam pointed to her stomach and asked what it was. I responded in a quivering voice, "Tummy," for at home we only spoke Spanish and what I spoke of English I mainly learned from the outside world and the other children at the daycare.

Mami covered all the papers required for registration with her long neatly written cursive lettering and we returned to our home. In reality, and in the law, I was a bit too young to enter kindergarten, for to enter you must be five years of age before the first of September, and my 5th birthday was not until October the 22nd, almost two months too late.

In order to avoid this problem mami did not submit my birth certificate, in the hope that the public schools would not mind nor ask to be given it, for surely then they would not acquiescently accept me. Three days later the school called, in need of the missing document, the document that would lead my parents and I through much pain that would not cease until I entered the grade in which I corresponded not by age yet by aptitude.

Upon knowing the decision of the school, my parents immediately began to oppose it by approaching the local authorities armed with letters of recommendation from two of my previous teachers, Mrs. Amanda and Mrs. Culpepper; mami and papi first conversed with Mrs. Neal, then the superintendent, and then the Board of Education. Each one of them spoke a long and soporific address, always ending in, "I'm sorry, but it's the law." My parents then decided to go beyond the local offices, and despite the fact that they knew limited English, they wrote letters to Governor Miller (the governor of Georgia), to the legislators, and finally, to President Clinton.

The following is a letter my father wrote concerning the issue upon us, in crude English, yet in marvelous sentiment and in great meaning:

OPEN LETTER TO THE PRESIDENT OF THE UNITED STATES OF AMERICA, MR. BILL CLINTON.
TO THE HONORABLE GOVERNOR MILLER,
TO THE HONORABLE LEGISLATORS OF THE STATE OF GEORGIA
AND TO THE BOARD OF EDUCATION OF CARROLLTON.

I'M SORRY, BUT IT'S THE LAW...

Gustavo Gac-Artigas

"I'm sorry, but it's the law..." the words resounded in my ears as a misinterpreted, misunderstood and recited poem by heart. In the end, depending on the category of the authority, they picked up a book with a green, red or black cover and recited aloud a paragraph; then added: "I'm sorry, but it's the law".

Since a month or a month and a half, more or less, I walked from one office to another, from the principal's office to the superintendent's, from the teacher's to the psychologist's and from there to the pharmacy in order to buy aspirins every time bigger and stronger to fight the increasing headache.

And, upon returning home we looked towards our little son who, in silence, with his expressive eyes, caressed his first grade books, those books which would turn him into a real student, those books he slept with, those books which opened the way to his young life, to life's secrets, to his father's dreams; those books which were beginning to offer him the basic tools for an apprenticeship, those books with which, for several weeks, he studied with love, and, in silence, with his expressive eyes. And in our ears the words still resounded... "I'm sorry, but it's the law".

And if I tell you all this it is because we were struggling to register our son Alejandro in kindergarten classes for 5 years old in the public school, because Alejandro's father is a writer, and not a president of any country, and he cannot afford to send him to study elsewhere.

Alejandro will turn five the twenty-second of October, because we conceived him in Holland and, therefore, we didn't know anything about the law and its deadlines, because we begotten him with love, without even looking at the calendar nor the law...

It is not fair, it is rather stupid, it is not useful. We agree with you that each child is unique and must be treated differently; we also agree that if a child is not performing at the right level he will become bored and turn into a bad student. He will get bored, as Alejandro got bored in the West Georgia College Campus Day Care Center, school he has attended for two years.

The Campus Day Care Center is excellent, but Alejandro needed to learn faster, and he expressed so. The director of the Day Care Center understood the problem and wrote a beautiful letter of recommendation on Alejandro's behalf, so he could be admitted to the kindergarten for five years old, and receive the necessary challenge that his intellect and eagerness for studying demand of him.

The piano teacher understood our child's predicament also, the very same person who has been teaching him music since he was almost four years old and who has followed his progress with great interest, and also wrote him an excellent letter of recommendation.

We too understood all this, but as we stated earlier, we know that for each parent his child is... and we asked, we begged, for him to be tested, we asked for a test that could determine if the child is or is not ready to enter school.

Because his father is a writer and not... Alejandro qualifies for a four years old kindergarten, a preschool program. Alejandro took a test, finally! And looking at the results the teacher said: "he is ready..., ready for the first grade, but the law..."

And everyone else added, sounding like a bad detergent ad, "why don't you send him to...? or to...?" And each to... costs around two thousand dollars... because the law says that to qualify for entrance to the public schools system you must be 5 years old by September the 1st, but.., oh! What a horrible suspicion might be crossing your mind as it crossed mine at that very moment! With money, in the private schools, you don't find that problem, the law doesn't exist, they will accept the child in agreement with his intellectual or financial capabilities, and age is not a problem.

And I've just said it, two thousand dollars I do not have, and beyond money matters, (and how difficult it is to think beyond money matters!) there's the law. "And to send him to a 4 years old kindergarten will be harmful to the child," said the teacher. The same thing uttered the specialist and the superintendent. And I agreed.

"The law?" Alejandro inquired, the law? "The law?" asked his sister Melina? What is the law useful for?

With lesser conviction in my voice, I told them: I suppose the law was made to protect children and not to safeguard this or that private enterprise; I told them that the law was written not to prevent children from registering in public schools but to guarantee that any child would not be excluded from them.

I imagine that the law penalizes citizens when a child is not sent to school, and should not prevent a child to attend school prematurely if he is prepared for it. If a deadline was chosen, it is to remind everyone that, at least from that age on, the children are protected by law, and their place is in school to learn about the world through the books, to be in contact with other children and teachers, and not in touch with inhuman work, abuse, and ignorance.

That's the reason for the law, I told them with conviction, to protect the children; not to punish them, to protect their development; not to stop it. Today, in a world in motion, science permits us to know if a child is ready or not to undertake his learning, and to know how can we help that child.

In a world in motion, to accept the opinion that there isn't anything we can do about it, that nothing will change, it means to accept a return to the Middle Ages. Let's not forget that in the past other people said exactly the same thing about other law and the law discriminated on the basis of color. And it wasn't fair. One day the law fell down; it was not easy but it crushed down.

If when writing the law the legislators forgot to write the thought behind it, why do they legislated for? If when interpreting it the law ties, and the law punishes, and the law does not protect, that law is not useful and it needs to be changed.

If barriers have fallen everywhere else, how can we not change the law, so that a child, with sadness in his heart, and questions in his eyes, should never have to ask his parents anymore: "why does the law forbid me to attend school if I want to, especially if the teachers say I can? They don't accept me. Why they don't accept me, papi?

And that a teacher or an authority should not ever have to say: "I've been struggling with this law for years, and I know it is not fair... Once I had a child whose birthday was in September 2, he was a gifted child, and my heart was bleeding, but there was the law, and for that reason he couldn't enter school. As you see, it is not fair but my hands are tied."

And if the law ties down a teacher's hands, it means that it prevents imagination and intelligence from developing as well. It means that the law is neither fair nor useful.

If we want life to walk in our children's eyes it is necessary to change the law or the law will destroy the confidence in the legislators, and in the public school, and in the law because the law..., the law...

We are sorry, but we didn't know about the law and we conceived Alejandro with love and not with law, because that law is not useful, because this law punishes the intelligence and the development of the children, the law is not useful for them, not useful for love, **and when the law is not useful you must change it,** and that's what I teach my children.

The answer:

OFFICE OF ELEMENTARY AND SECONDARY EDUCATION
JULY 9 1993 THE ASSISTANT SECRETARY

Mr. Gustavo Gac-Artigas
126 F Danny Drive
Carrollton, Georgia 30117

Dear Mr. Gac-Artigas:

This is in response to your letter to President Clinton regarding the age requirement for entrance into public school.
I read your letter with great interest and I understand your concern. However, State and local education officials have the responsibility and authority over the operation of our public schools. Therefore, I encourage you to contact your Chief State School Officer in Georgia. For your reference, he is:
Dr. Werner Rogers
Superintendent of Schools
State Department of Education
2066 Twin Towers East
205 Butler Street
Atlanta, Georgia 30334

Thank you for writing.
Sincerely,
A signature

The response we were directed led us once again to the point where we had begun: the local authorities, the response of Carrollton, Georgia. Not knowing how to react, my irresolute parents returned to

Mrs. Neal, and pleaded for her assistance. Mrs. Neal stated that perhaps I should attend a private school until second grade, for the law did not state a certain age one must have to enter the grade.

At that point my parents were near collapsing, for during research they discovered that private schooling cost minimally two thousand dollars a year. How in the world were they going to pay for two years of private schooling at two thousand dollars a year if even then they were seeking to move to another apartment complex because they couldn't afford the rent at Cedar Villas anymore?

I suppose Mrs. Neal, who was a very intelligent and understanding person, read my parents' thoughts and she ventured to suggest: "I know that Alejandro is perfectly capable of attending first grade," she stated, "but as you know, my hands are tied by the law. This is the best I can do: I will lend you all the books and material we use here for first grade, and you can homeschool him. At the end of the year we will give him some tests, and if he passes them, which I don't doubt, he can enter second grade in this school."

It's impossible to describe mami and papi's great elation, there are no words capable of describing their joy when they returned to the apartment, to home. I asked them, "Why don't they like me? I will be a good student; I just want to learn!" My papi took me in his arms and *me dio vueltas en el aire* while my mami said *"te quieren Alejandro,* they love you, in one year you will be at the 'big school'. We have a whole year to prepare you for that big moment."

I was baffled by those contradictory words, on one hand she was telling me that they loved me, and on the other she said I had to wait a year. Nevertheless, their smiles, their gleaming eyes and visages, which I had not seen for quite a while, since the point when the entire issue of my education began, were telling me to trust them.

All my parents had intended to do was to enter me in kindergarten, yet they did not have an option. They visited the three private schools of Carrollton asking for some sort of "scholarship". The best proposal they would hear was to pay only half of the tuition and the other half would be subtracted in exchange for mami to give Spanish classes to the children from first to fourth grade. Eventually we moved to an apartment complex both more pleasant, and cheaper, we shrunk our grocery and clothing expenses, and so we managed to spare one thousand dollars, and I was sent to The School of the South.

The School of the South was a small,

mostly partisan, religious school. It contained lifeless cold tiles, and was educationally limited. (The great majority of the teachers there also happened to be mothers of students who attended.) I was the only *Latino* in the entire school, and utterly proud. With the exception of kindergarten, each room contained two grades which were taught on the same level, although were assigned different homework for English and Math. In the case of science and other classes, the students were all given the same assignments.

The classes contained about twenty students each, both boys and girls. There were two playgrounds, one for the younger children, and one for the older. They were separated by a large metal fence which reached just above my head. The main objective of the youngest children was no longer to rest atop a tower or something of the sort, it was to have the possibility to play on both sides of the fence.

It was in this instance which I once again felt imprisoned, as the gorillas at the zoo, as the boy on the leash. Previously, my parents had spoken to the kindergarten teacher of The School of the South. She was corpulent and overweight, although very pretty and affectionate. Mrs. Richards, her name, believed I was prepared to enter first grade, and so she conferred with the teacher of the grade, Mrs. Forester. After much quarreling, I was allowed to enter first grade.

At this very early age in my life as a student, I learned the importance of being loved and accepted by a teacher in the process of learning. Until that moment, I had been loved by my teachers: Miss. Jill, Miss. Kim, Mrs. Amanda, Mrs. Culpepper. Mrs. Forester accepted me in the classroom, but she never accepted me in her heart. As I stepped into the classroom of the first and second graders, I felt a certain fretfulness come about me. At that point I told papi, who was accompanying me, to not leave, to stand in the back and watch me. He promised to do so, although he later left. The class began well, yet but minutes after it commenced, I turned and saw papi had left, and broken his promise.

Mrs. Forester had little patience for children, much less for me, which was ironic for she had a son of my age. So intimidated was I by her screams and yells that I didn't dare to breathe, so as not to disturb her. I could not concentrate, and I wept. The other children were sympathetic towards me, for they understood that she was attempting to rid the class of me. Perhaps she, being both a teacher and a mother, was jealous, for her son remained in kindergarten and I was younger than him and yet in a higher grade.

In any case, she stated my crying, which was by all means her fault, was a distraction for the other children, and so placed me in the desolate hallway and shut the door. A wooden sign on the door, with "Mrs. Forester" carved upon it quivered. Forlorn, I wandered to the wing to which Mrs. Forester had briefly explained to go. Another sign above the passageway read "kindergarten." I was appalled and offended; I believed that perhaps, in the din, I had misheard her directions, yet before I fully pondered the issue, Mrs. Richards opened the door and ushered me inside, as if expecting me. At the moment the other children were taking a nap upon colored mats.

Mrs. Richards told me to pick a spot and rest for the little time left of sleep. I chose a red mat, which was my favorite color, near the mat of a small blond-haired fragile girl named Addie. Thinking of all that could happen, I cried, attempting to stifle my sobs, for they seemed so prominent in the utter silence. Addie rose and silently walked to me, stepping over sleeping children, to the corner of the classroom where a large box of tissues lay. She took a tissue, cautiously returned to her mat, and outstretched her hand gesturing for me to take it and dry my tears.

In not long my stifled sobs turned into stifled laughs, for as Mrs. Richards passed by me, a gust of wind blew through the opened window and lifted her skirt. Instead of panties she wore a pink towel because of her tremendous size. I was the only child awake, and so the only witness of the incident.

When in the afternoon my parents asked Mrs. Forester about my class she responded with a smile: "he cried, he didn't finish the work, he disrupts the learning process of the other kids". My parents expected Mrs. Forester to praise me, to be joyous I was in her class, to care for me. Seeing that Mrs. Forester was no longer going to accept me in her class, they returned to Mrs. Richards, the kindergarten teacher who had been willing to teach me, who told my parents, "I did not know it was going to be like this. Please, leave him here with me, for I have another girl that is also very advanced and I will teach them both first grade here in the classroom."

This was precisely what mami and papi did, but of course her first grade lessons were quite insufficient, for she had a kindergarten group to tend to, and so, upon reaching home in the afternoon, after school had concluded, yet before going outside to play with my sister Melina, my parents took the books we had received from Mrs. Neal and began to home-school me, began to teach me first grade far better than anyone else could. Each night, papi and I had math contests, most of which I won. And so, I learned the times tables, able to recite them with the snap of a finger and the blink of an eye. In what seemed like the same amount of time, my days at The School of the South passed, and I was more than prepared to enter second grade.

THE EXAM

Because of the fact we had averted in a certain way the law, Mrs. Neal had to be certain I was prepared to enter second grade. And so, present at the school at the time we arrived were numerous specialists from Atlanta, psychologists, educators, etc. to test my knowledge, abilities, social development, and all what they thought was necessary to perform well in second grade.

The great number of experts, and Dr.'s, and people with PhD's produced mixed feelings within me. I was both anxious and frightened, both clear-minded and confused. In not long I was called into a room containing several people who remained silent, observing, and a woman who asked questions. After about an hour of oral testing the written portion of the exam was given to me, which I was to finish in the remaining two hours.

I later learned I was being tested with extremely difficult questions for the age, some of which reached fifth grade. Subsequent to the three hour exam mami and papi, having saved a bit of money, took Melina and I to have lunch at the nearby, newly installed restaurant, Chick Fillet.

We awaited the results for two endless weeks. As the third week following the exam commenced, we received a phone call from Mrs. Neal asking us to appear at the school as soon as possible. Melina and I waited outside the office of the school holding hands. My sister has always been present when I needed her most.

In but short moments, my parents emerged, carrying Mrs. Neal's statement that she had no doubt that I was ready for second grade. She said that now all she would have to do was to find among her 2nd grade teachers the one who would be best for me; one that did not reject me for my age and who desired to teach me. In her mind she thought she knew precisely who the teacher we were in lack of was, but the teacher must have to agree in the first place.

Mrs. Neal left us with the anticipation of awaiting her telephone call. We later returned home, with yet another night without rest, waiting, waiting for the telephone to ring, waiting for a yes.

The next day, at approximately the same time we arrived at the school, we received a call from Mrs. Neal informing us that the instructor she had in mind had accepted. . . her name was Mrs. Scott. At 5 ½ I was going to be the youngest second grader in her class.

Mrs. Scott was a middle-aged woman with short curly hair, which was at the time graying, of reddish, blond, and brown shades. Her parents were German, yet she spoke with neither a German nor Southern accent. Mrs. Scott taught with an assistant "paraprofessional" teacher, Mrs. Campbell, as did the majority of the other teachers. I had always found Mrs. Campbell's Georgian accent amusing, but irritating for she continually attempted to make my "pretty" into "*pertty.*"

On the first day of class, and my commencement of being educated at Carrollton Elementary, I saw the children from the Campus Daycare awaiting the teachers in the first grade aisle. As I passed, a mother of a child I had known in the daycare, after seeing me walking towards the section for second grade, said, in an unsuccessful attempt to belittle and laugh at me, "Are you lost? Kindergarten is that way," she pointed her slender finger in the direction of the kindergarten section of the school. I responded, "No, I know exactly where I'm going. . ." I pointed my finger, mimicking hers and stated "to the 2nd grade."

She followed me with her eyes and stared in disbelief as she saw Mrs. Scott welcome me to the class. Before the door of the classroom closed behind me, I turned and saw her. She stared at the wall, stoic, with no expression upon her face, wearing the same pale mask I had seen so often, mouth wide open.

In Mrs. Scott's class were twenty-six children, all of whom I had never met, yet most of which I befriended within the first semester of school. My first and most amiable friend in the classroom was a girl named Traprina. Traprina was of average height, was thin, and upon her face wore a partially toothless smile. Wavy blond hair hung a bit below her shoulders. Other classmates and companions were Erin, a small black boy who always displayed his two golden teeth, Megan, a thin and cautious brunette, Charlie, Sarah, Samantha, Cedric, and numerous others whom I came to know as the school year progressed.

Mrs. Scott accomplished what Mrs. Neal had asked of her; to accept me as I was, a *Latino* boy with great desire to drink the world; she taught me, and cared for me, and significantly solicited me to go reach farther than reality. She always emphasized for me to write creatively. In fact, it was Mrs. Scott who created the base upon which I wrote this book, and for that I am truly grateful. It was during the time period in which she taught me that I wrote my first story, which received first prize in a contest organized by *Carrollton Connec-*

tion, a local paper, and was published in the following edition. I was also mailed a letter of congratulation from the publisher of the weekly paper.

The story I wrote is entitled . . .

"What It's Like to be a Baseball"

by Alejandro Gac-Artigas
Second Grade
Carrollton
Elementary School

One day I said, "I wish I could be a baseball". The next day I WAS a baseball!

I was worried. What would I do? I had an idea. I would run away. Then I realized I couldn't walk.

So, what could I do? I would have to think of another idea. I thought, and thought and thought. Then I had a new idea: I would ROLL away to the baseball field!

The next day the baseball players found me. What would I do now? They kept hitting me back and forth! It was HORRIBLE!

But one night I finally sneaked across the yard and rolled as fast as I could until I got home. Then I opened the door and sneaked by my mom who was washing dishes.

Then I rolled up the stairs, opened the door to my room and quickly wished I was myself again.

The next day, I think I wished I was a BAT!

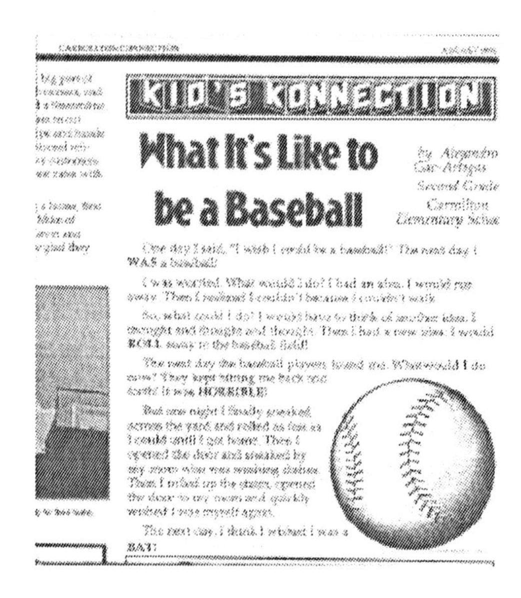

KID'S KONNECTION

What It's Like to be a Baseball

by Alejandro Gac-Artigas
Second Grade
Carrollton Elementary School

At that moment, though I did not realize it, I first entered the magical world of writing.

MY SISTER, MELINA

Melina's hair falls just below her narrow shoulders, a glamorous black shade. The tips slightly curve inwards encircling in her face. Gleaming eyes peer below her eyebrows, and above her thin, pale lips. She is of neither tall nor short stature, and is extremely intelligent. Beyond having classmates and companions Melina has befriended Leo, a doll, whom we cherish, and now carries our last name, Gac-Artigas. Leo is in fact of more age than Melina, although she delineates a newborn baby. I have learned greatly from Melina, and so am much more wise in my actions during the course of my life.

Melina once wrote a poem that I will remember always, in which she expressed her thoughts:

You are...
yourself
your thoughts
your dreams
You are different.

She wrote this poem, being that we were *Latinos*. I find great admiration for she was not ashamed of difference.

WOODGLEN APARTMENTS

To be able to afford the fee The School of the South presented, we moved to a cheaper yet more refined apartment complex, known as Woodglen apartments. It contained much more land than Cedar Villas, the apartment complex in which we previously lived, a pool, and a large forest. More importantly, it contained Whitney, the best companion I have ever had to this date.

The apartment we rented was composed of two stories. It was for the most part carpeted with the exception of the kitchen and bathroom. In the center of the living room laid a television collecting dust, for Melina and I did not often watch. Our room, Melina's and mine, was found to the right of the staircase leading the second floor. As one entered the room they would see two twin beds laying parallel to each other in the far corner. To the left was a closet which served to store our piles of toys. The toys sat in boxes to which we had glued various colors of cloths in patterns and pictures. For instance, upon one was a young girl made of pink and blue cloths, and so on.

Both the toys and boxes created an array of colors which seemed as if having the capacity to belittle the rainbow. The boxes were arranged in a manner so as the opening faced outwards. The structure Melina and I created reached far above my head, so I was barely ever able to play with the toys on the top floor of what seemed like the cross-section of a large building.

The boxes we used to store the toys were hallowed, containing immortal memories from two separate lands. It was these boxes that we used to move from Puerto Rico to America. They brought all our things that would fit within them. Presently we have many possessions dispersed among relatives and in countries we previously lived. Someday I wish to have the possibility to return to Holland, Puerto Rico, France, and all the countries where I may find the objects that hold our past and history.

Approximately fifteen feet to the left of our apartment was the forest. Its trees towered to great heights, and were draped in an unbroken regalia of leaves, its roots embedded in the red dirt of Georgia. The first tree of the forest, nearest to the apartment, Melina and I named Mr. Tree. This tree, unlike any other in the forest, was a pine. Mr. Tree stood to be about one foot tall when we arrived. When we left he was almost twice my height.

It seems as though my life was determined by weather phenomena; at my birth there were great winds, and as we arrived at Woodglen apartments, an immense snowstorm struck. I was quite a novice to the snow, although it was present in Holland, since we had recently come from Puerto Rico, where winter temperatures do not fall below seventy.

Being that I had never gone sledding before, I asked mami and papi to take me. They reminded me we had no sled, yet I stated that it did not matter for we could make one. My parents agreed and in not long had created a sled made of cardboard and rope. I was overcome by joy, as was Melina. We marched to a nearby lake with a hill alongside it, and sledded until the cardboard wore thin.

WHITNEY, THE BEST OF FRIENDS

Her name was Whitney Phillips. She was three when I first met her. She was five when I last saw her. Whitney was the daughter of the woman who owned the apartments, our landlord, Lynn. Her hair was almost purely blond, and fell to about her shoulders. She was a trifle shorter than me, and was younger than me by a year. Her birthday was within the first days of October while mine was on the 22nd.

Whitney had glistening green eyes, accompanied by a wonderful smile. She was a bit bossy, yet nevertheless caring and amusing. Whitney was audacious and courageous, but once she was given the opportunity to prove her lack of fear, it seemed to appear.

I first met Whitney while practicing the piano. She heard the music and meandered about the area until she arrived at our apartment, from which the music came. Whitney softly tapped the door a number of times until papi opened it. She asked who played the piano and upon hearing my age asked if when I finished I could play with her. Papi said yes. And so I met Whitney, the best of friends.

To Melina and I, Lynn, Whitney's mother, grew to be the aunt we did not have, for all our relatives were elsewhere, and to Whitney, Melina and I grew to be the siblings she did not have, for her brothers and sisters had grown and were also elsewhere. Lynn had no lack of money and was able to bring us to movies and restaurants, to the city, to come to know the luxuries of Georgia. Each time she invited us to a restaurant we simply asked for a sandwich and water, or something of the sort, being accustomed to order only what mami and papi could afford.

Whenever it was possible for my parents to spare money, they took the opportunity to invite Whitney, to attempt to repay what Lynn had so easily done. They gave Whitney a choice: either an ice cream or a happy meal. She accepted the terms without uttering a phrase but "Happy meal, please." She wore a tremendous smile upon her lips. Though perhaps we may not have had as heavy wallets as they, Whitney cared for us, and in return for her care we present her with the most valuable gift of all: We will love her always.

MOVING AGAIN

Not long after the great snowstorm, mami returned from the college quite gloomy, in fact. She turned to papi and spoke to him in a barely audible voice. They told us they would be going for a walk, which they always did when problems were upon them. Previously they would simply speak French, which at the time we could not understand, yet Melina and I had begun to decipher their meaning, and so they now took walks alone. We did not dare to follow.

Melina and I craved the knowledge of what had happened, yet we feared the knowledge, feared the fact that when they walked it meant eating bread and water for a week. The problem that burdened us was worse than what I had thought was the worst . . . mami lost her job.

For a long while mami had strived both night and day, attempting to receive a PhD, for with it the college would promote her to assistant professor. The college would then have to raise her paycheck by at least ten thousand dollars, and it would be "the end" of our financial problems. Mami and papi began to search for a house to buy. The accomplishment signified we would be able to pay the bills, and perhaps buy me a new bicycle. Mami became Dr. Priscilla Gac-Artigas as December concluded. It was our only Christmas present. In but days the college received notice of mami's doctorate, and because of what the college stated were funding shortages her position as an instructor was cut out and her contract was not renewed.

Wasting no time, we began to search for opportunities in which mami would rightfully teach as a professor. Each response we received was situated in a far-off state. We would take out an ancient map of The United States, and find the state on the map. Following several replies, mami received one in the North which she found quite favorable. My small finger fell on Sycamore Hills, a suburb near New York, and at that moment I knew that it would be there where we would now live.

In the one hand the North meant the free concerts in Central Park, the ones that we used to watch on TV in Georgia in which I fell in love with Pavarotti's O Sole Mio; it meant to be close to our Tio Ado, the only family we had in the United States, yet it also meant to leave Whitney and Lynn, the only friends we had, to leave Mrs. Neal's school, where I was accepted as a second grader, and worst of all it meant to be uncertain, to start all over again.

A TEARFUL GOODBYE

As the month of August commenced, something more significant ended. It was in these first days that we would say farewell to the South and greet the North with great expectations. The previous night Melina and I had begun to remove the embellishments from the boxes and once again place our few belongings within. These boxes had held our things for many previous moves, and would for this one as well.

I turned and looked at the apartment one final time. Papi shut the door. The sound seemed to echo in my mind. I had finally begun to accommodate to Georgia, to the apartment, and all was taken in the simple closing of a door. Mami traversed the hill of our backyard, and handed the key to Lynn. A tear rolled down her cheek.

The following night we slept, or more correctly put, attempted to sleep in a furnished apartment Lynn had lent us, for all we had was contained within the painted walls of a Ryder truck. Earlier, Lynn and Earl, her husband, had brought us to a Mexican restaurant called "The Lazy Donkey" to begin to say farewell, and so our stomachs were full with the most refined food of Georgia, and our eyes with the most precious tears.

In the morning, we finished packing the few things still left and drove to Whitney's home. We said our final goodbyes, yet Whitney was not present. As we left, I saw Whitney quivering beneath a desk crying. I also broke to tears and ran to our worn Ford. Mami turned on the radio and playing was Pavarotti and O Sole Mio. I dried my tears and simply sang, lamenting the loss of Whitney, the best of friends.

THE SUBURB

The university in which mami would now work assisted us in finding a house we could rent for a small price. We came upon a light blue house alongside a large road, Hope Rd. The house was situated near the school which had been said to be excellent. The university where my mother now taught, laid but minutes from where we had moved to, Sycamore Hills. Sycamore Hills is a miniscule town, borough, in fact, located extremely near the ocean, and once on summer days one can hear the winds of the ocean, and smell the salinity of the air.

The first task we performed, after going to the beach, of course, was to register me in the school I was now to attend: Sycamore Elementary School. The principal of the school was much as Mrs. Neal, middle-aged and ever so caring. Upon meeting the principal, we handed her a folder which Mrs. Neal had previously given us. It contained not only my report card, but a detailed list of all I had studied and which books I had used. I was then placed in a third grade class taught by a woman named Mrs. Keller.

Also in the same year I developed a

love for soccer, playing for a small town team. I had always wanted to play soccer, and did with Melina, using a ball of tied cloths, yet in Georgia the sport was both not known and hence not played or appreciated. At each game, the entire team of children ran wherever the ball had come to be, as if engraved in the leather were diamonds.

September commenced, as did my schooling in Sycamore. I was immobile with fear, petrified, both anxious and yet afraid to set foot in my new school, in which I knew no one. For brief moments, while walking upon the sidewalk, hand in hand with mami, my fear became so tremendous I lost sight, viewing only small dots waltzing about a pale white background.

Mrs. Keller, unlike Mrs. Scott, and very much like Mrs. Forester, did not pay any attention to me in the classroom. She pelted my feelings, and attempted to make me feel as if I did not belong within her classroom's walls. Throughout the first days in her class I reminisced of Mrs. Forester, for in Mrs. Keller I saw the same hatred in her glasslike barren green eyes. Each day, after school concluded, mami asked, *"Hijo, cómo te fue en la escuela hoy?"* I responded with, *"Bien,"* saying that school had gone well, although it had not been true. I lied for I wished to *pelear* this battle on my own, and I was not going to allow Mrs. Keller to send me back to second grade, for I had won with great effort my position in third grade, and nobody could take that away.

Each night my eyes filled with tears of disbelief, for I had done nothing wrong. I had been respectful, and had studied until I memorized definitions word for word, but still yet Mrs. Keller threw upon me the most dreadful feeling of being insignificant. She would neither speak nor even glance at me. Each day she would greet each child as they entered the classroom, yet as I walked by, in the hope that perhaps Mrs. Keller would speak to me as well, she simply looked towards the next child and welcomed him. And each morning I woke, knowing that Mrs. Keller would care for me as much as she had the day before, yet still wishing she may have changed.

I believed in order to win the respect and care of a teacher should take nothing more than to be a good student. Although until that time the concept proved fallacious, I began to study until I fell asleep, for endless hours I studied upon my wooden desk, which now had the forms of letters I wrote imprinted within, and I slept there with my pencil, now worn to a stub, in my small, red, aching fingers. My head lay on the papers covered in the lead of my pencil, and when I woke, I was able to read what I had written, for the ink had been marked upon my face. I washed my face until the soap diminished significantly in size, and it now wore the lead. In my eyes one could see I had not slept, yet also there was a shield of determination.

When Mrs. Keller asked me to use our vocabulary words in sentences I would write sentences of two or three lines, describing both whimsical and sophisticated issues which I believed would be approved by Mrs. Keller. They were not. They were erased and replaced by "Sam ran home." My sleeves were draped in chalk, yet the blackboard was now bare. Mrs. Keller did not even speak a word of approval, yet neither did she criticize. I saw that as an indication that perhaps she may have been changing her ways. She was not. I received hundreds on my vocabulary tests and still yet she said nothing.

Once I had studied until midnight for an exam. The exam was on social studies, and I was more than prepared to take it. I felt as if this may be the day in which Mrs. Keller would care for me as I expected. I entered the classroom and though she did not greet me, I still felt assured once she saw my paper all would change.

Being extremely nervous, I had forgotten to remove a sheet of paper from my backpack before placing it in the closet. As I stood to fetch it, Mrs. Keller asked what I was doing. I told her that I had left the sheet of paper in my backpack, and inquired in a polite manner if I may go and get it. She responded telling me to sit down and that I would receive a "zero" on the test. I sat, not knowing, irresolute, unsure of whether to cry or complain, while the other children took the exam. In front of all my classmates she sat me down and denied my wish. At that moment I realized she had not changed.

As I returned from school I wept until I had no tears to weep, and bearing my tears no longer, mami and papi told me they were going to speak with either Mrs. Keller or the principal. I did not want them to go, for I, being my obstinate self, stated it was my battle and mine alone. I desired to fight alone and win alone. But that night, Julianne's mom, a French girl that was in my class, called my parents and asked them if they were aware of what was happening in the classroom. She told them Julianne wept every night and had asked her, "How can she be so mean to Alejandro who is so sweet."

The next day I woke just as any other day, and expected what I had expected just as any other day. Mrs. Keller taught just as any other day, and she neglected me just as any other day. I felt terrible just as any other day, and my efforts were slain, just as any other day. As the day concluded, unlike any other day, I was called to the office. I felt a bit nervous although I knew I had done nothing wrong.

As I walked down the hallway everything seemed to become quiet, the yells of the children faint and far off. My breathing and footsteps were the most prominent sounds. In not long I reached the passageway leading the office. Engraved upon the door was "Mrs. Bloomfield," and beneath it, "Principal". I unwillingly yet instinctively opened the door. Inside sat a secretary behind large rimmed glasses typing. She said hello. The word seemed as if a foreign concept, and it had been so long that I did not hear it that for a moment I forgot what the response should be. Overcome by joy I said hello with a great gap-toothed smile.

The secretary told me in a high-pitched tone to go into the next room. I followed her pointed finger and reached the partially rusted door knob. I was unwilling the open the door, fearing what awaited me on the other side. In seconds I brought up courage, and as I inhaled, opened the door. I saw mami and papi, Mrs. Bloomfield, and Mrs. Keller.

I expected to be spoken to by only the principal or my parents, yet then came a voice directed towards me. Though it was neither the tone of my parents or the Principal I glanced at them for I thought it to be impossible for Mrs. Keller to speak to me, yet as I turned my head I saw Mrs. Keller with her mouth ajar speaking to me in an unstable but soft tone.

It was the first time she had spoken to me, and though I had heard the voice many of times in the past, it seemed completely different. She sat me on her lap, so I could feel her breath, which was extremely warm compared to her heart, and began to speak to me. Her make-up was a bit smeared and so I reasoned she had been crying, and her green eyes were full with an ocean of tears.

Mrs. Keller pleaded for me to pardon her because of all she had caused. Though a trifle doubtful whether I should or not, I forgave her, and gave her a hug. It was as if her tears washed away her coldness and bitterness, for she seemed truly sorry. In a firm but soft voice, while still embracing her I asked her why? Why had she pretended as if I did not exist? Why did she not commend me for my great efforts? Why did she never greet me? and so forth.

The explanation Mrs. Keller presented was that she thought that by ignoring me in the classroom she was doing me a favor, believing that being young, I did not want much attention. Mrs. Keller told me between breaths and tears, that we would begin over. I did not believe the explanation was truly genuine, just as her saying "Tomorrow's a brand new day," yet I sprang at the opportunity to begin once again, correctly. Leaving the office, mami and papi told me that she would no longer be unjust. I responded, "you didn't see her eyes;" it was her eyes that told me she had not changed as much as I had wished. It was her deep green eyes that told me that part of her coldness had not been washed away by their tears.

Bit by bit Mrs. Keller began to change her ways. Her eyes no longer showed traces of bitterness. Her smile no longer seemed as if it had been forced to appear. She greeted me warmly with both words and expressions as I entered the classroom, and it seemed as if she appreciated my work. Not only was she more amiable with me, but with all the children. She was no longer the "witch" she had come to be known as, although some children did not realize.

I had won the battle, not alone as I had wished, yet it was won and nothing could be greater than that. She was more lenient yet taught very well. Once, being still not yet assured that Mrs. Keller had in fact altered the manner in which she behaved, I was under the impression that Mrs. Keller was attempting to trick me. The directions of an exam I took stated to circle the letter before the correct answer. I smiled, for I was certain it was a trick, and so I marked the letter before the letter of the correct answer. For instance if the correct response was "D," I marked "C," and if the correct response was "C," I simply marked "B." The tricky thing, I thought, was when the correct answer was "A"; I promptly marked "D".

Having thoroughly studied for the exam, assured that I would receive an A+, I left Sycamore Elementary feeling both wise and victorious. The next day, after school had concluded, Mrs. Keller asked to speak with me. My small ears awaited praise and commendation, yet heard something quite different. She told me I had received a "zero," she emphasized and articulated the number, on the exam, and stated that I was not the type of student to receive such a grade.

I explained to Mrs. Keller how I believed it was a trick, and how I marked the response before the correct one, as I interpreted the directions. My smile was now of humiliation. Mrs. Keller laughed and laughed, then the laughs were accompanied by tears, and finally she kissed my forehead and brushed my hair aside, telling me that it was no trick. As she corrected once more my paper, Mrs. Keller found that I had answered each question correctly, and gave me the A+ I knew and she knew I deserved.

This incident was the commencement of a long-lasting bond of both care and fidelity. As the school year concluded, Mrs. Keller recommended me for the most advanced classes of fourth grade. Each summer I see her at the library, say hello, and we converse as if we had known each other for ages, for I will never forget her, and hope she will never forget me.

SYCAMORE JUNIOR HIGH

Once again I was to leave my school and attend another, yet unlike the times this had previously occurred, I would not lose the classmates I had come to care for, nor the area I had come to love. Both my classmates and I, would now attend Sycamore Junior High, the school that I had mentioned to appear in my future, for the fourth grade, the grade in which we corresponded, stood to be the commencement of a separate school holding 4th, 5th, 6th, 7th, and 8th grades. It was a sort of promotion, to "the big school," just as to attend kindergarten one would have to say farewell to the Campus Daycare and greet Carrollton Elementary.

The school year of third grade concluded, and as by tradition, Sycamore Junior High held a welcoming assembly in its auditorium, at the time both the gym and cafeteria as well, where the children who had arrived to Sycamore Junior High that year sung melodies telling us not to be afraid and to be bold and audacious.

Sycamore Junior High stood to be a fairly sized school. The hallways were thin and small, so as not to allow much movement in the minutes between classes. Each day after lunch they reeked of sweat.

For the great majority of the children of fourth grade, the most important possession of Sycamore Junior High was a locker, for only the children of 6th grade and higher had the great honor of receiving them. As my years in Sycamore Junior High passed I gained possession over locker 238 which I thought would be an advantage, yet posed as a threat.

My locker stood between two very similar lockers, yet the owners of the neighboring lockers and I were not at all alike. Each day I dreaded going even near my locker, fearing the two children next to it. Being that the lockers had little room between them, children would be touching shoulders with each of the students on either side of them. As I would approach my locker, both my legs and hands quivered, for I knew that the moment my hand touched the black dial it would be thrown aside, and my ears would hear the so often used words, "Me first."

Papi always was curious why each day after school had concluded I came home either bruised from attempting to be courageous, or late from being a coward. I never told him. Not until the last moment did I tell papi, for it was almost certain he would talk with the principal, who was almost certain to speak with the children, who were almost certain to "speak" with me. The two students would open my locker, place my coat and possessions upon their backs, and run about the school.

In the morning I would arrive at the school and find my coat in the water fountain and books thrown about the hallway. I would arrive late at my classes and would be punished. Still yet I told no one of the issue, which seemed as if a waste of breath for each child of the grade were very aware of what was occurring. Some confronted other similar problems, and some created them. My back became quite sore for I would carry all of my books within my backpack, so as to avoid walking even near my locker. In the night mami would sew my book bag which had torn from the weight.

Each year, being that the lockers were grouped by grade, I received a locker closer and closer to the 8th grade wing, the lair of the most notorious children of Sycamore Junior High. The walk to my locker reminded me of a picture I had once seen in my science textbook of a large fish fighting the current of a river. It seemed as if each day my outstretched fingers were but inches from the dial, yet at that moment I would be pushed back another foot. I would wait until few children remained scampering about the hallway, staring with frightened eyes, and then began the walk to my locker. Instead of being a great joy, the locker posed as a great enemy.

In not long, jokes began to arise, racial jokes, of *Latinos*, of hatred. As I walked in the hallways I would hear someone speaking words which would tear apart my heart: Mexican "spic" Spanish. They where meant to be jokes, to amuse, yet they did in fact discriminate against a number of people, human beings. A child once spoke these words to another, by my side, so I could hear: "Mexicans can have expensive bikes because they can steal them. They live in cheap houses because they can't steal a house." Though I am not Mexican, that day I felt as if I were.

It was this incident, and mami's refined fingers worn and punctured by the needle, which made me realize that this could go on no longer. And so came "the last moment" in which I told papi what had, and still occurred. Between tears of both pity and disbelief, he told me he would speak to the principal and that this would abruptly stop. Each tear stung my heart as if acid. I could never bear papi's tears.

QUIET PLEASE. SPELLING BEE

Because of my grades, I had come to be in the highest levels of both Language Arts and Mathematics, and so was very pleased with my academic achievement, yet others looked down upon me in my English class for they thought I didn't belong there. In fact, a mother entered our home, to congratulate my parents because of my high placement and progressed to ask how they were going to help me with my work, for as the year progressed the work would become increasingly more difficult. I read in her green transparent eyes what she was thinking; it seemed as if she were almost hoping that I would not be able to follow the rapid pace of the class.

Each year she would ask mami and papi how I was performing in my classes, and each year she left with the response that I had done well. At that moment I promised myself that I would strive not only to attend the highest classes, but to become the best in each.

Night and day I worked to perfect my English, much as I had done in third grade. "Da" became "the," and the notion that I was not able to succeed vanished.

Upon commencing classes, Mrs. Allen, my fourth grade teacher, announced that in not long there would be a spelling bee held by Sycamore Junior High, and that being in the most advanced courses we had a great chance of winning.

I could see in each of the children's eyes that they believed they would win, and that they just cast me aside as the one without possibilities of winning. From that moment on, I did not rest until I had memorized the spelling of words whose spellings I did not already know, until I had learned lists and lists of spellings and definitions, tenses and grammar.

One morning I woke with a list before my eyes, just as any other day in the past weeks, yet the morning was somehow different, and I could not quite recognize why. I finally realized, as I walked towards the school, that it was the day of the spelling bee. My footsteps increased until it appeared as if I was in a stage between walking and jogging, for I wished not to be late, and to have a small period of time to review the list.

Throughout mathematics it seemed as if my eyes stared both at the spellings and at the revolving hands of the clock. For a brief moment in my anxiety I was almost certain they had pointed to the list, gesturing for me to continue and I did, yet I later realized the time had changed and the hands had simply moved to the correct hour. As I blinked my eyes, now weary from each spelling, the bell rang, announcing that in but minutes the spelling bee would commence.

Each child walking towards the class wished to be the first, yet nevertheless they paced themselves attempting to display their calmness, nonchalant assurance that they would win. I myself was not quite as concerned in my appearance, simply reviewing the most difficult spellings in my mind.

By the time I reached the class I was a bit dizzy, yet more importantly, prepared. I turned my head and saw children walking about with lists and papers. Others did not care about the spelling bee and did not desire to win. Of the twenty-one children in my class only about five had an opportunity of winning.

To the great majority of the children I was not included in the small number of prepared students, yet I was, and I knew it. After reviewing countless words and definitions, I reached a quite familiar door upon which a sign had been taped. It read "Quiet Please. Spelling Bee. Thank You."

As I read, a strange sense that I had seen something unthinkably horrid crept up my spine. At the time, in my mind, I believed it to be much, much worse . . . I had arrived. I now stood before the room in which I must have gained victory and proved to the other children that being *Latino* shouldn't be a stereotype telling that they were not capable of speaking or spelling as well as Americans.

In not long I began to hear, faintly, the footsteps of my classmates walking towards me. I peered into the window and saw Mrs. Allen behind spectacles, sitting alongside her desk, reading papers. A bit relieved, I entered the room and took my seat. I tapped my small fingers upon my wooden desk and awaited the commencement and completion of the spelling bee.

Mrs. Allen arose from her position at the paper-covered desk, and called the now full class to silence. She explained to us the rules of the spelling bee: We would all stand and once we misspelled a word we would sit and watch the rest of us in silence. We could ask Mrs. Allen to repeat a word or use it in a sentence. To clarify the rules we were given a period in which we would ask questions and secure our doubts.

The correct manner to spell a word was to state the given word, spell it, and repeat the word once more. Once one began to spell a word they could not begin again and change what they had already spelled. If any of the rules were broken, the opportunity of winning was broken as well. Perhaps I had no doubts and so asked no questions, yet most likely I was too frightened to speak. And so the spelling bee began.

In the first few rounds little misspellings were heard, few children sitting. Just after the first child fell, many others also began to spell incorrectly, and so the spelling bee moved rapidly. At each time in which a child sat, I felt quite awkward, with the same sense I had experienced as I beheld the sign upon the classroom door.

The number of standing children became smaller and smaller until only one remained . . . me. From then, gaining a name as "the walking dictionary", I proceeded to the school spelling bee and from there to the district spelling bee where I lost, in the final round, to the word criticize.

As I returned to our small blue house, I wept until I had no more tears to weep. I knew the word, I had spelled the word the previous night while preparing for the spelling bee. Mrs. Hayes, once my math instructor, stated that I had misspelled the word for I was never criticized.

These words also led to the title of me being a "teacher's pet," which led me to perform some "mischievous deeds" that banished the name from my reputation. It was that day that mami and papi bought me a Franklin Speller which has sat by my side each moment in which I read a novel and has since greatly bettered both my spelling and vocabulary.

I FAILED

The Plus Test was an exam given by Johns Hopkins as a portion of the university's "talent search." Only a selected few were allowed to take the exam, those who had scored higher than a 97 on the tests given by Sycamore Junior High as the school year concluded. In the small number of selected students I stood in pride.

Once again I began to study madly, perhaps I studied too much, or as I took the test I was overcome by both fear and apprehension, or perhaps I over-thought each problem, yet in any case I failed, not by much, but I failed. It was as if someone had taken a jar containing my heart and shattered it upon the floor.

Every child and adult seemed as if they had expected the results I received, just as they expected for me not to excel in most aggressive classes, as if saying he finally fell as we knew he would, for he is a young *Latino* boy and can do no better. In their eyes I saw their laughter and satisfaction, and I expected for them to plead for an article to be written in the paper mentioning the children who had received higher scores than I, their sons. They would waltz about the town showing each pair of eyes, the photograph of their children in the paper, and would make sure that it was known that my face was missing.

I was aware that in the following year would come a similar exam, also given by Johns Hopkins University, an exam used as a portion of the decision as to what college a student may enter. . . the SAT. As the date in which I was to take the SAT arrived, I stood to be prepared, my mind strangely quite calm and composed. I was led to a small room at the end of a meandering hallway. A woman sitting behind the pages of a book titled "How to Guide the SATs" stared at me for a moment and told me to take a seat for we would soon begin. I chose to sit in the first row near her, where I could clearly hear her voice. About me sat children both twice my height and twice my age who were to take the exam to enter college.

The instructor called the class to silence and we took the exam in a period of more or less three hours. As I left the classroom I said farewell to the guide and though I wished to run into papi's arms, I walked calmly about the hallway, at the head of a great mass of students, and only awaited the arrival of the results. When mami and papi asked me how I had done I told them neither badly nor well, for when the same question had been asked to me the previous year, I responded very well, but the results told quite the contrary. In but weeks my scores arrived in the mail. I had received an 1100. Of 1600 I had received 1100 at the age of eleven. I was a bit disappointed, yet it stood to be the highest score of the grade. Although no parent pleaded for there to be my photograph present in the paper, I was recognized in both an awards ceremony given by the school and honored by the state in a ceremony for children who scored highly on the SAT. I had succeeded.

THE OTHER SIDE OF TOWN

As I strolled down the deserted streets,
The golden Thanksgiving sun setting in the west,
My cold, numb ears centered on "thank you's" of the wealthy side of town.

"Thank you for my toys", rejoiced the young children.
"Thank you for my cars, and Cuban cigars."
"Thank you for my jewels", chimed the women.

Suddenly I stumbled upon a conspicuous change,
Not only in wealth, but also in what was uttered.

"Thank you for the sun that warms me.
Thank you for my parents, who brought me into this world.

Thank you for my few precious friends,"
Were the solemn words of the other side of town.

. . .

The rest of my walk was spent in melancholy, on the verge of tears.

How could the two sides of town be so distant?

This question may remain unanswered for eternity.

LITERATURE

While I was in the 6th grade my interest in literature began to significantly grow. I began to write more often, write longer papers, read more difficult novels. I no longer wrote the length the teacher asked of us nor used words that I saw as not sufficiently sophisticated. My Language Arts instructor saw my avidness to write and read further and to be of academic excellence. Not long after I first set foot in her classroom mami and papi received a call from Mrs. Emerson, the teacher. She was asking for permission to take me further in both reading and writing; mami and papi gladly gave it to her.

As the year concluded I looked back upon the moments in her class, and saw that I had read books meant for high school students, had written poetry that made tears fall down my cheeks, which I had read along with students from a university at a poetry reading I had been invited to.

All my poems I gathered and placed in a small book which I titled *Call of a Raven*. I dedicated the book to my Tio Ado, who had passed away the previous year. He was the only relative I had in the United

States. Never before had I encountered the death of a relative I truly knew and cared about. Tio Ado remained my only friend in America from the time in which we arrived to the time of his death.

After writing about half of the book, ideas for poems became rare, and so I wrote some of past or present endeavors. "The Other Side of Town" I wrote this poem based upon John, a child in my grade who was even poorer than I, and was laughed at because of the misfortune.

John lived in the other side of town. Every child seemed as if to ridicule John in some way or another: perhaps deriding the helmet he wore, made of Styrofoam and string, perhaps of his orange bicycle with no brand whose squawking would be heard whenever John began to pedal, perhaps because they considered him not as intelligent as them, yet they could never laugh at his heart, for though it was wounded from the many vulgar words spoken of him, it was pure, something no amount of money could buy. Children even dared to throw the food John had been given by the school upon the ground asking him if he had paid for it. He would eat nothing that day.

I once saw John riding his bicycle about the street. He came across a child walking his dog. John stopped and stroked the dog, asking what kind he was. The child responded inquiring why he cared, for his father did not have the money to buy him one. John once again mounted his bicycle and left. Each word directed towards him would on almost all occasions be armed with a weapon to puncture his heart, and by the expression on John's face it seemed as if it caused me more pain than he, for I had been in a similar situation and knew that if one did not leave it within their past it would suffocate them and leave them almost completely destroyed and powerless. John did not leave in time.

One year John did not return to school in September. Some said he and his mother had moved to Newark, the city, and now lived by the smokestacks. Others stated that he could no longer afford the rent of his small house and now lacked one. I once saw John quite a bit of time later. He had come to watch the fireworks on the 4th of July, by the river. He wore upon his back the same clothes I had last seen him in, the clothes so familiar yet so distant, worn so that in some areas all that separated John's back from the air were but strings.

I did not ask John where he now lived and what it was like. I did not want to know. I was frightened of the response I knew would cause great pain, would revive past memories I wished to remain there, would cost me the number of tears each child in Sycamore Junior High owed him. I just hugged him, and we watched the fireworks together sharing a red, white and blue cotton candy.

Though perhaps John was in debts of money, they stood to be in greater, more important debts of pardons.

SOCCER

I remember as I ran towards a goal with the recess soccer ball alongside my feet, years ago how I sat alone upon a cold metal bench, only watching the soccer I wished to be participating in. The soccer team whose uniform was upon my back, yet whose list telling players what position they were to play did not contain my name. I did not remember playing, such a wonderful luxury, simply sitting frozen as winter paid its visit, numbed from the cold, viewing those playing as I wished to do so, such a terrible, horrible burden.

In front of me stood a rather large boy, one many years older than I in age. It was not the first time I had seen him, and I had neither said nor done nothing to offend him, and so perhaps I should not have been frightened, yet his size and more importantly his cold gray eyes alarmed me. Along with the ball I moved towards the right, attempting to pass around him. I was lifted by the might of his arms, far above the ground to my eyes, and dropped so my head would be to hit the ground . . . I lost all visible signs of consciousness.

My eyes saw nothing but the seemingly eternal dark, my ears heard the distant calling of my name, Alejandro. The voices tapered off into a somewhat familiar voice calling the name of other children and positions. I began to regain sight yet I did not see faces above mine, still calling my name. Beneath my foot was a soccer ball, yet not the recess ball. And, yes, about me stood children, yet not the ones I had last seen. The children were dressed in uniform, all wearing the exact attire with the exception of numbers and names inscribed upon the back. They were dressed in a uniform I had worn many times before, yet had never done what I was to do within it.

In not long, no longer able to bear the sense that my eyes had seen what they now saw once before, I recognized that what my eyes, or perhaps my mind now viewed was quite a time ago, the same day I had reminisced of, as my soccer coach assigned position to each child. The better you played in the practices the more time you played in the games, used to say the coach.

I practiced whenever I was able to, in the streets, in the parks, at my house, and every practice bettered. After each practice I was certain I would play in the next game, even saw for a moment in the coach's eyes that he would assign me a position on the field. Nevertheless, as the team practiced, but minutes from the commencement of each game, the coach would not speak to me. My ears awaited to hear what position I was to play, but his eyes were staring in the direction of the next child. To the other children who would not start the game, he would tell them they would not be playing immediately, yet to me he did not speak a word.

He didn't place me in the game, or even tell me I was not to play, as if I did not exist. The coach then told the team to take their positions. I would ask myself to go where. I would tell myself that he had simply forgotten to give me a position. I would take a place upon the bench. So after several games when he neared me, I began to fear what I knew was to occur yet was reluctant to acknowledge that in but moments I would take my "unassigned" position . . . the sidelines.

Each time a child was taken out of the game, I eagerly stared at the coach, for perhaps I would take his place. He entered another child not even glancing at me. From time to time I would stand by his side, to remind him that I was there, thinking once again that perhaps he had forgotten. The coach simply walked in a different direction and began to speak with another child. Too hurt to further attempt to be placed in the game, I bleakly walked back to the bench.

I could no longer move or feel my toes, numbed from the cold. I would jog in place so I would be able to even perform such a simple yet necessary task . . . breathing. Cold was all I would allow to enter my mind. Cold and the dim hope that perhaps I would play a bit of the game. I later wrote in Mrs. Emerson's class a story which, though I never told anyone, was in fact based upon my thoughts and sentiments as I sat upon the bench of terrible memories.

Alejandro Gac-Artigas
Language Arts

A Day to Die

Cold. That was all the man would allow to enter his mind. Cold and death. It had already been five days since his eyes caught a glimpse of something other than the unbroken whiteness stretching on endlessly, or his ears hearing something outside of the occasional call of a lonely bird suffocating in its solitude and the roaring bellow of three feet of snow being mortified under his feet. Then, he vowed never again to return to the icebound lands. Alaska, to him, was just a myth, a figment of his imagination he was inspired to believe in. Yet all was gone. Life. Hope. Everything. And where was he? Who knows.

The sun was setting, and the sky losing its paleness to a brilliant golden brown. The sky, as if a blazing flame, shone through all evil. Wild colors roaming freely, waltzing about the arctic sky. Yet this was only a small flicker of hope in his heart, quickly fading. He was losing the battle of the frost.

Cold had overcome the man, and he was running blindly, in his delirium, while visualizing illusions of his past. A blur of images spinning faster and faster, as if he were dancing and twirling through time. The ballad of illusions. And, and, and he returned to reality, bewildered, gasping between breaths. It was his first of many hallucinations to come.

Snow was coming down in sheets now, shielding his eyes from the real world. A curtain as if of pure silk hiding from view the world he was so used to. Enclosing the man in what was to be his coffin.

Cold was playing with the man's mind now. Illusions coming and going, as if flipping through the family photo album. All his past was revealed in front of him. Reliving what he had already lived, and then it was gone. Just like that. All gone in one split second. The magic disappearing trick. Then, the man knew it was still to come one final time. And to think, all this from cold.

Just penetrating the numbness was the feeling of cold. Cold like he had never experienced before, some seventy-two degrees below zero. And then he knew it was time to build a fire. As he struck the match, he knew there must be no failure for it was his only match, and lit the bark in flames, his eagerness overcame him. The man dropped the match, still alight, in the snow. The fire was out. And so was the small flicker of hope in his heart. Then he lay still in the snow, waiting for death to pass over him. His adolescence. His kin. His death. With that, the lonely traveler took his final defeat, and death prevailed over his body. And he knew, it was a day to die. It certainly was a day to die.

Each time the cold reached beneath my skin and crept up my veins I would think of the coach's heart, for when I thought of it, the bench upon which I sat then, seemed quite warm.

The assistant coach had a somewhat kind heart and knew that I was not the sort of player to sit the entire game on the bench. He knew that by the way I played in the practices I had won my position in the games yet was not given it, and he desired for me to play nearly as much as I did. He would place me in the game time and time again, and I would scamper onto the field. At that moment the coach would say, "Alejandro, out," ridiculing me in front of the eyes of both my teammates and their parents.

Each game I would be entered and then immediately taken out in but moments. During those few moments I felt the coach's eyes upon my back, grasping me and pulling me out of the game. My legs felt extremely heavy, as if I wore fetters, and the cold began to suffocate me. I then heard the coach's voice calling me out of the game.

That fear of the coach's voice, all the children on the team had, we were terrified of his shouts and directions and criticisms, and so while on the field we all wore the same fetters of fear which barely allowed us to move our legs. What would further wound my heart was the realization that I stood to play no more than minutes in the entire time I wore the team's uniform upon my back.

To some extent I had a privileged position on the sidelines, able to see both near and far. In the far distance I saw parents, which seemed as if bundles of cloth, for they wore hats upon hats, and scarves and mittens, and coats and sweaters and boots. Each breath they took was followed by a cloud of grayish fog, as if dragons who had run out of fire.

I myself was far, far colder than they, only wearing my uniform. I had a jacket in my bag, yet did not wear it attempting to silently tell the coach I was warm and prepared to enter the game. The only result I received from this action was a cough. In front were playing children. I wished to be among the players and not to watch them from afar.

Even before them stood a screaming coach, red with fury, for the team was losing the game. His veins were defined upon his bald head. In his eyes was a burning flame of wrath. When he called a name, it sounded as if an insult, yet even so, I wished it was my name he was calling, calling to enter the game. I heard the voices of parents, voices attempting to encourage and not criticize. The faces seemed farther and farther away, while the cold became larger.

Still lying upon the ground viewing the world with my eyes shut, I saw the faces of Mrs. Forester and Mrs. Keller before she became a dear friend; I saw, years later, a girl waiting by her coach's side, and not being spoken to, and a boy sitting upon another bench, a part of another team, with another coach, yet with the same cold I felt years in the past.

An arm reached out for me from a forest. It was my mother's. She grasped mine and told me that we were to leave the soccer field. As it approached it seemed a savior, yet when it arrived I recognized that once I left, I was never to return, for I would certainly be thrown off the team. I once again sat down and told mami that next year would be different.

As I lay upon the soccer field I saw children entering a restaurant to celebrate the final game of the season. I heard a voice that told mami and papi, "Alejandro is no longer part of the team. He will not return next season. Oh yes, we need his uniform." With a cold smile upon his face, and barren eyes the coach offered me pizza. I ate but one piece, the most bitter slice of pizza I had ever eaten.

That night I practiced in the backyard until I collapsed with no more force. I slept embracing my uniform. The next morning it was not in my arms.

Voices seemed to very slowly approach, and a certain warmth came over me. A hand reached to me, a voice apologized, and asked me to rejoin the team. Yes, this year things were to be different, the sun was rising.

I opened my eyes and found myself lying upon a somehow familiar soccer field. I stood and brushed the dust from my back, and going back to school I realized that, perhaps, they do not love me, but they must take me into account, for I exist.

Yo, Alejandro.

September 17, 2000

Other Titles Published by

Ediciones Nuevo Espacio

Novela, cuento y poesía

Ado's Plot of Land
Gustavo Gac-Artigas - Chile
Benedicto Sabayachi y la mujer stradivarius
Hernán Garrido-Lecca - Peru
Beyond Jet-Lag
Concha Alborg - Spain
Buenos Aires
Sergio Román Palavecino - Argentina
Como olas del mar que hubo
Luis Felipe Castillo - Venezuela
Correo electrónico para amantes
Beatriz Salcedo-Strumpf - Mexico
Cuentos de tierra, agua.... y algunos muertos
Corcuera, Gorches,
Rivera Mansi, Silanes - Mexico
El dulce arte de los dedos chatos
Baldomiro Mijangos - CDLibro- Mexico
Exilio en Bowery
Israel Centeno - Venezuela
La lengua de Buka
Carlos Mellizo - Spain
La última conversación
Aaron Chevalier - Spain
Los mosquitos de orixá Changó
Carlos Guillermo Wilson - Panama
Melina, conversaciones con el ser que serás
Priscilla Gac-Artigas - Puerto Rico
Prepucio carmesí
Pedro Granados - Peru

Rapsodia
Gisela Kozak Rovero - Venezuela
Ropero de un lacónico
Luis Tomás Martínez - Dominican Republic
Simposio de Tlacuilos
Carlos López Dzur - USA Latino
Todo es prólogo
Carlos Trujillo - Chile
Under False Colors
Peter A. Neissa - USA
Un día después de la inocencia
Herbert O. Espinoza - Ecuador
Viaje a los Olivos
Gerardo Cham - Mexico
Visiones y Agonías
Héctor Rosales - Uruguay

Academia:

Caos y productividad cultural
Holanda Castro - Venezuela
The Ricardo Sánchez Reader / CDBook
Arnoldo Carlos Vento - USA

http://www.editorial-ene.com
ednuevoespacio@aol.com
New Jersey, USA

9 781930 879218